Beginner's Sourdough

Easy Everyday Sourdough Bread Baking

Contents

easy sourdough bread 1

sourdough bagels 4

sourdough breadsticks 7

jalapeño cheddar sourdough 10

cinnamon raisin bread 13

soft sourdough dinner rolls 17

homemade croutons 20

sweet potato rolls 22

sourdough hamburger buns 25

einkorn sourdough bread 28

sourdough hawaiian rolls 31

sourdough country loaf 34

soft sourdough pretzels 37

pull apart cheese bread 40

slow cooker sourdough bread 42

sourdough french toast 45

sourdough english muffins 47

honey wheat sourdough sandwich bread 50

sourdough ciabatta rolls 53

sourdough berry sweet rolls 56

gluten free sourdough bread 59

easy sourdough bread

PREP TIME: 10 mins · COOK TIME: 50 mins · FERMENTATION TIME: 8 hrs

Ingredients

INGREDIENTS TO MAKE ¼ CUP (50 G) OF ACTIVE SOURDOUGH STARTER
2 teaspoons (10 g) sourdough starter
3 tablespoons (25 g) all-purpose flour
5 teaspoons (25 g) water

DOUGH INGREDIENTS
¼ cup (50 g) active sourdough starter (100% hydration)
1 ⅓ cups + 2 tablespoons (350 g) water
2 teaspoons (10 g) fine sea salt
4 cups + 2 tablespoons (500 g) bread flour

Instructions

FEED YOUR SOURDOUGH STARTER
12 hours before you plan to mix the dough, add the ingredients to make ½ cup (100 g) of active sourdough starter to a clean jar. Stir until combined, loosely cover the jar and let the starter rise at room temperature. (The ingredients will create a total of 115 g active starter but, because some of it will stick to the sides of the jar during the transfer, we are making a little more than needed.) The sourdough starter is ready to use when it has doubled in size and there are plenty of bubbles on the surface and sides of the jar.

1

MAKE THE DOUGH

In the bowl of a stand mixer, stir together the starter, water, honey and salt with a spatula. Add the bread flour and use your hands to bring the ingredients together as best as possible. The dough will be very stiff. Place the dough hook on the mixer and mix the dough on the lowest speed for 6-7 minutes. (Or 10 minutes by hand.) Cover the bowl and let rest at room temperature for 8-12 hours. (See notes for cinnamon raisin bagels.)

Line a baking sheet with parchment paper. Turn the dough out onto a clean work surface and divide into 8 equal pieces. Shape each piece into a ball. To shape the bagel, place a dough ball on the surface in front of you and use your thumb to poke a hole straight down through the middle of the dough.

Pick the bagel dough up, gently shape the ring and place on the parchment paper. Repeat with remaining dough balls. Cover the dough with a towel and let rise for 30-60 minutes or until puffy. (See notes about parchment paper.)

Preheat oven to 425°F (218°C) making sure that the oven rack in the center position. Bring 6 cups of water to a boil in a large stockpot and add 1 tablespoon of sugar. Once the bagels have finished rising, boil them for 2 minutes on each side. (Only boil 3-4 at a time, making sure not to crowd the pot.)
Use a mesh stainer to remove the bagels and let rest on the parchment paper until cool enough to handle. Once cool enough, dip one side into your choice of toppings and place back onto the parchment paper.
Bake the bagels at 425°F (218°C) for 25-28 minutes or until golden brown.

sourdough bagels

PREP TIME: 25 mins · COOK TIME: 35 mins · FERMENTATION TIME: 12 hrs

Ingredients

INGREDIENTS TO MAKE ½ CUP (100 G) OF ACTIVE SOURDOUGH STARTER
1 tablespoon (15 g) sourdough starter
⅓ cup + 1 tablespoon (50 g) all-purpose flour
3 ½ tablespoons (50 g) water

BAGEL DOUGH
½ cup (100 g) active sourdough starter
1 cup + 1 tablespoon (255 g) water
2 tablespoons (40 g) honey (or sugar)
2 teaspoons (10 g) fine sea salt
4 cups + 2 tablespoons (500 g) bread flour

WATER BATH
6 cups water
1 tablespoon granulated sugar

OPTIONAL TOPPINGS
sesame seeds
Everything Bagel Seasoning
salt (sprinkle on top, don't dip)
poppy seeds
shredded cheese

Instructions

FEED YOUR SOURDOUGH STARTER
12 hours before you plan to mix the dough, add the ingredients to make ½ cup (100 g) of active sourdough starter to a clean jar. Stir until combined, loosely cover the jar and let the starter rise at room temperature. (The ingredients will create a total of 115 g active starter but, because some of it will stick to the sides of the jar during the transfer, we are making a little more than needed.) The sourdough starter is ready to use when it has doubled in size and there are plenty of bubbles on the surface and sides of the jar.

MAKE THE DOUGH
In the bowl of a stand mixer, stir together the starter, water, honey and salt with a spatula. Add the bread flour and use your hands to bring the ingredients together as best as possible. The dough will be very stiff. Place the dough hook on the mixer and mix the dough on the lowest speed for 6-7 minutes. (Or 10 minutes by hand.) Cover the bowl and let rest at room temperature for 8-12 hours. (See notes for cinnamon raisin bagels.)

Line a baking sheet with parchment paper. Turn the dough out onto a clean work surface and divide into 8 equal pieces. Shape each piece into a ball. To shape the bagel, place a dough ball on the surface in front of you and use your thumb to poke a hole straight down through the middle of the dough. Pick the bagel dough up, gently shape the ring and place on the parchment paper. Repeat with remaining dough balls. Cover the dough with a towel and let rise for 30-60 minutes or until puffy. (See notes about parchment paper.)

Instructions

Preheat oven to 425°F (218°C) making sure that the oven rack in the center position. Bring 6 cups of water to a boil in a large stockpot and add 1 tablespoon of sugar. Once the bagels have finished rising, boil them for 2 minutes on each side. (Only boil 3-4 at a time, making sure not to crowd the pot.)
Use a mesh stainer to remove the bagels and let rest on the parchment paper until cool enough to handle. Once cool enough, dip one side into your choice of toppings and place back onto the parchment paper.
Bake the bagels at 425°F (218°C) for 25-28 minutes or until golden brown.

Notes
This recipe was tested in a 68°F (20°C) kitchen. If your kitchen is colder, rising times will take longer and if it's warmer, less time.
If using all-purpose flour reduce water to 325g. Add more if necessary during first set of stretch and folds.

This bread can be baked in a lightly greased 9" x 5" loaf pan. After the first rise, shape the dough, place it seam-side down into the loaf pan and allow it to rise. Bake the loaf in a 375°F (190°C) oven for 45 minutes or until the internal temperature is 190°F (88°C).

sourdough breadsticks

PREP TIME: 10 mins - COOK TIME: 20 mins - FERMENTATION TIME: 8 hrs

Ingredients

INGREDIENTS TO MAKE ½ CUP (100 G) OF ACTIVE SOURDOUGH STARTER
1 tablespoon (15 g) sourdough starter
⅓ cup + 1 tablespoon (50 g) all-purpose flour
3 ½ tablespoons (50 g) water.

DOUGH INGREDIENTS
½ cup (100 g) active sourdough starter
¼ cup (56 g) butter (room temperature)
2 tablespoons (42 g) honey (or sugar)
1 cup + 2 tablespoons (270 g) water
2 teaspoons (10 g) fine sea salt
4 cups + 2 tablespoons (500 g) all-purpose flour (or bread flour)

GARLIC BUTTER
3 tablespoons butter
2 cloves garlic (crushed)

Instructions

FEED YOUR SOURDOUGH STARTER

12 hours before you plan to mix the dough, add the ingredients to make ½ cup (100 g) of active sourdough starter to a clean jar. Stir until combined, loosely cover the jar and let the starter rise at room temperature. (The ingredients will create a total of 115 g active starter but, because some of it will stick to the sides of the jar during the transfer, we are making a little more than needed.) The sourdough starter is ready to use when it has doubled in size and there are plenty of bubbles on the surface and sides of the jar.

MAKE THE DOUGH

Mix the dough: Add the ingredients to a large mixing bowl and bring them together with your hands. Turn it out onto a clean work surface and knead the dough by hand for about 10 minutes. It will become smooth in texture when it is ready. (If the dough is sticky, lightly dust your hands with flour as you are kneading but don't add too much. It will become less sticky as you knead it.)

Stand mixer instructions: Combine the dough ingredients in the bowl of a stand mixer fitted with the dough hook attachment. Mix on medium speed for 8-10 minutes. The dough will become smooth and pull away from the sides of the bowl when it is ready for the next step.

Bulk Fermentation: Cover the bowl and allow the dough to rise 50-70% at room temperature.

Shape and Second Rise: Divide the dough into 12 equal portions, each should weigh approximately 80g. Use your hands to roll each portion into a log shape. Line two baking sheets with parchment paper and arrange 6 breadsticks per sheet leaving space for them to rise. Cover the sheets with clean tea towels and allow the dough to rise until they are puffy and risen by 30%

Score and Bake: Preheat your oven to 400°F and bake the breadsticks for 20 minutes. Garlic Butter: Heat the butter and crushed garlic cloves in a small saucepan while the breadsticks are in the oven. Remove the breadsticks from the oven and brush each one with warm garlic butter.

11

jalapeño cheddar sourdough

PREP TIME: 40 mins · COOK TIME: 50 mins · FERMENTATION TIME: 12 hrs

Ingredients

INGREDIENTS TO MAKE ½ CUP (100 G) OF ACTIVE SOURDOUGH STARTER
1 tablespoon (15 g) sourdough starter
⅓ cup + 1 tablespoon (50 g) all-purpose flour
3 ½ tablespoons (50) water

DOUGH INGREDIENTS
½ cup (100 g) sourdough starter (active)
1 ½ cups (360 g) water (30 grams divided)
⅓ cup + 1 tablespoon (50 g) whole wheat flour
3 ¾ cups (450 g) bread flour
2 teaspoons (10 g) fine sea salt

ADD-IN INGREDIENTS
¼ cup (60 g) sliced jalapeños (pickled or fresh)
4 oz. (113 g) sharp cheddar cheese (shredded)

jalapeño cheddar sourdough

PREP TIME: 40 mins · COOK TIME: 50 mins · FERMENTATION TIME: 12 hrs

Instructions

FEED YOUR SOURDOUGH STARTER

12 hours before you plan to mix the dough, add the ingredients to make ½ cup (100 g) of active sourdough starter to a clean jar. Stir until combined, loosely cover the jar and let the starter rise at room temperature. (This will create a total of 115 g active starter but some of it will stick to the sides of the jar during the transfer, so we are making a little more than needed.) The sourdough starter is ready to use when it has doubled in size and there are plenty of bubbles on the surface and sides of the jar.

MAKE THE DOUGH

Autolyse: In a mixing bowl, combine 330 grams of water and 100 grams active sourdough starter, stir to combine. Add 50 grams whole wheat flour and 450 grams bread flour and use your hands to combine the ingredients until there are no dry bits and the dough looks like a shaggy mass. Cover the bowl and let the dough rest on the counter for 1 hour.
Add salt: Add 10 grams of salt to the remaining 30 grams of water in a small bowl and stir to dissolve. Add the salt water to the dough and use your hands to work it in until well combined. Cover the bowl and let rest on the counter for 1 hour.

Bulk fermentation: Perform 3 sets of stretch and folds, 30 minutes apart, over the first hour and a half. Add the shredded cheddar cheese and jalapeños to the dough during the second set of stretch and folds. Keep the bowl covered between sets. Once finished with the third set of stretch and folds, cover the dough and allow to rise at room temperature for an additional 2-3 hours. (Alternatively, you can cover the dough and let it rest in the fridge for up to 36 hours.)

How to perform a set of stretch and folds: While the dough is still in the bowl, pick up one side with a wet hand. Pull it up and over itself. Turn the bowl and repeat this action on 4 sides of the dough until the bowl has come full circle.

Shape and Second Rise: Turn the dough onto a floured surface and shape into a rough ball. (The outside of the dough will not be smooth). Flour the top of the dough and place into a floured proving basket, top-side down. Allow to rise at room temperature for 2-3 hours or until it has risen about 20%-30%.

Preheat: Preheat the oven, with the dutch oven inside, to 500° for 30 minutes.

Score and Bake: Turn the dough out onto a piece of parchment paper and score the top with a razor. Remove the dutch oven and place on stove-top. Use the parchment paper as a sling and lift the dough up and into the dutch oven. Cover with the lid, turn oven down to 450° and bake for 30 minutes. Remove the lid and bake an additional 20-25 minutes or until the crust is at the desired color.

Cool: Let the bread cool on a cooling rack for 2 hours before cutting.

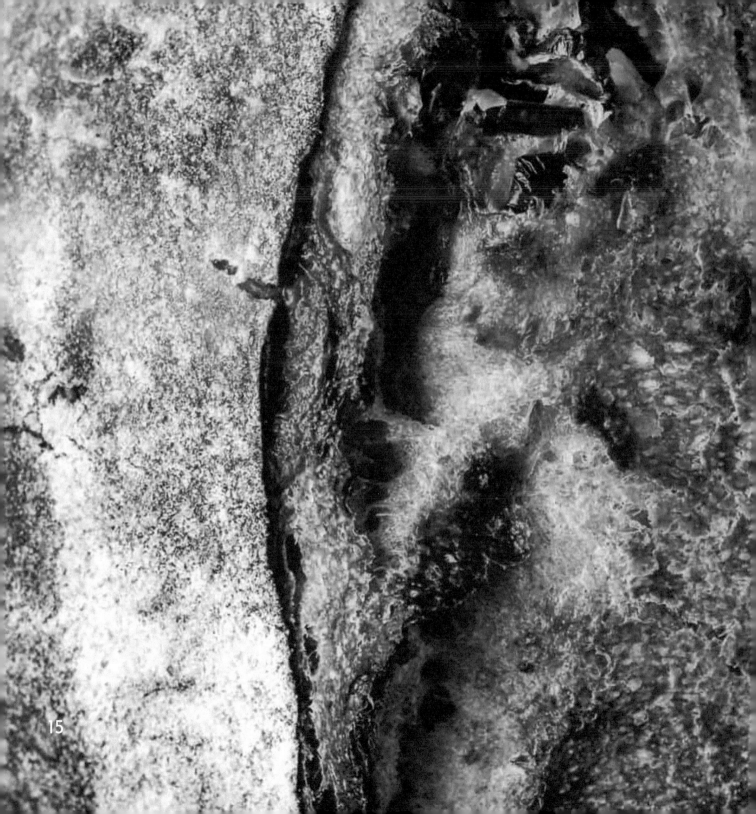

15

cinnamon raisin bread

PREP TIME: 30 mins · COOK TIME: 50 mins · FERMENTATION TIME: 1 day

Ingredients

INGREDIENTS TO MAKE ½ CUP (100 G) OF ACTIVE SOURDOUGH STARTER
1 tablespoon (15 g) sourdough starter
⅓ cup + 1 tablespoon (50 g) all-purpose flour
3 ½ tablespoons (50 g) water

DOUGH INGREDIENTS
½ cup (100 g) active sourdough starter
1 ½ cups + 1 tablespoon (375 g) water
2 teaspoons (10 g) salt
3 ⅓ cups (400 g) bread flour
⅓ cup + 1 tablespoon (50 g) whole wheat flour
⅓ cup + 1 tablespoon (50 g) rye flour
ADD-INS
½ cup raisins
½ cup walnuts

CINNAMON SUGAR FILLING
4 tablespoons butter (room temperature)
¼ cup brown sugar
2 teaspoons cinnamon
½ teaspoon vanilla extract
pinch of nutmeg

Instructions

FEED YOUR STARTER

12 hours before you plan to mix the dough, add the ingredients to make ½ cup (100 g) of active sourdough starter to a clean jar. Stir until combined, loosely cover the jar and let the starter rise at room temperature. (The ingredients will create a total of 115 g active starter but, because some of it will stick to the sides of the jar during the transfer, we are making a little more than needed.) The sourdough starter is ready to use when it has doubled in size and there are plenty of bubbles on the surface and sides of the jar.

MAKE THE DOUGH

Mix the dough: In a large mixing bowl stir together 100 grams of active sourdough starter, 375 grams of water, and 10 grams of salt. (This step will ensure the starter is evenly distributed throughout the dough.) Next add 50 grams of whole wheat flour, 50 grams of rye flour, and 400 grams of bread flour to the bowl. Use your hands to combine the ingredients until there are no dry bits and the dough looks like a shaggy mass. Cover the bowl and let the dough rest on the counter for 1 hour.

Prepare walnuts and raisins: While the dough is resting, prepare the raisins and walnuts. Bring a small pot of water to a simmer and turn the burner off. Add ½ cup of walnuts and ½ cup of raisins to the pot, making sure they are covered by the hot water. Allow them to sit in the hot water until it's time to mix them into the dough.
Stretch and fold: Perform one set of stretches and folds to the dough. To perform a set, while the dough is still in the bowl, pick up one side with a wet hand. Pull it up and over itself. Turn the bowl and repeat this action on 4 sides of the dough until the bowl has come full circle. Cover the bowl and let the dough rest for 30 minutes.

Add walnuts and raisins to the dough: Drain the water from the raisins and walnuts and then add them to the bowl of dough. Use your hands to mix them into the dough until they are evenly incorporated. Cover the bowl and let it rise 30-50% at room temperature, 3-5 hours depending on the temperature of your kitchen.

Prepare butter spread: Right before the dough is ready to shape, mix 4 tablespoons of softened butter with ¼ cup of brown sugar, 2 teaspoons cinnamon, ½ teaspoon vanilla extract, and a pinch of nutmeg. Set aside.

Spread butter mixture on the dough: Turn the dough out onto a floured work surface. Use your hands to press the dough out into a 12 x 10" rectangle. Flour your hands to prevent the dough from sticking. Spread the butter mixture over the dough being careful to keep it 1-1 ½ inches from the edges.

Shape the dough: Pick the right side of the dough up and fold it towards the center and repeat with the left side. Pick the top side up and fold it towards the center and repeat with the bottom side. Fold the dough in half and then flip it over so that the seam-side is facing down. Pull the dough towards you while turning it to create a taut skin on the outside. Dust flour on the outside of the dough and flip it into a lined banneton that has been floured. Cover the banneton with plastic wrap.

Second rise: If you'd like to bake the same day, allow the dough to continue to rise at room temperature until it has reached the top of the banneton. For a long ferment, let the dough sit on the counter for 30 minutes before placing it in the fridge overnight.

Bake: Preheat your oven to 450°F (232°C) with a dutch oven inside. Once the oven is hot remove the dutch oven and set it on top of the stove. Turn the dough out onto a piece of parchment paper. Use a razor to make 3 very shallow slits across the top of the dough. Using the parchment paper as a sling, lift the dough up and into the dutch oven. Bake covered for 30 minutes and uncovered for 20 minutes.

Cool: Place a cooling rack onto a piece of parchment paper or baking sheet. (This will catch any melted butter that may drip from the baked loaf.) Transfer the loaf to the cooling rack and allow it to cool completely.

18

19

soft sourdough dinner rolls

PREP TIME: 15 mins · COOK TIME: 30 mins · FERMENTATION TIME: 8 hrs

Ingredients

INGREDIENTS TO MAKE ½ CUP (100 G) OF ACTIVE SOURDOUGH STARTER
1 tablespoon (15 g) sourdough starter
⅓ cup + 1 tablespoon (50 g) all-purpose flour
3 ½ tablespoons (50) water

DOUGH INGREDIENTS
2 tablespoons (28 g) butter
1 cup (240 g) milk
3 tablespoons (44 g) sugar
1 teaspoon (5 g) salt
½ cup (100 g) active sourdough starter
3 cups + 2 tablespoons (375 g) bread flour
1 tablespoon melted butter (for brushing the top of the rolls after baking)

Instructions

FEED YOUR STARTER

8 PM Feed starter: 12 hours before you plan to mix the dough, add the ingredients to make ½ cup (100 g) of active sourdough starter to a clean jar. Stir until combined, loosely cover the jar and let the starter rise at room temperature. (The ingredients will create a total of 115 g active starter but, because some of it will stick to the sides of the jar during the transfer, we are making a little more than needed.) The sourdough starter is ready to use when it has doubled in size and there are plenty of bubbles on the surface and sides of the jar.

MAKE THE DOUGH

7:30 AM Melt butter: In a small saucepan, melt the butter, milk, sugar and salt together over low heat. Pour the mixture into a mixing bowl and allow it to cool down to room temperature.

8 AM Mix the dough: Add the flour and active sourdough starter to the bowl and stir with a spatula until the ingredients are combined and there are no dry bits left in the bowl. Cover the bowl and allow to rest at room temperature for 1 hour.

9 AM First rise: Perform 3 sets of stretch and folds spaced 30 minutes apart, keeping the bowl covered between sets. To perform a set, pick up the dough on one side and stretch it up and over itself. Turn the bowl a quarter turn and repeat this step until you have turned the bowl a full circle. After the final set, cover and allow the dough to rise for 2 hours or until it has risen by 50% in size.

12 PM Shape and Second rise: Turn the dough out onto a floured surface and divide it into 12 pieces, approximately 65 grams each. Shape each piece into a ball by gathering up the sides and pinching them together. Turn the dough over so that the seam side is down on the work surface and gently form a smooth ball. Arrange them in a lightly greased glass baking dish. Cover the dish with a tea towel and let rise for 3-4 hours.

4 PM Bake: About 20 minutes before you are ready to bake preheat your oven to 375°F (190°C). Bake for 25-30 minutes or until they are golden brown on top. The internal temperature of the rolls should be 190°F when fully baked. Brush the top of the roll with melted butter and serve.

Notes

It's very important to take the ambient temperature of your kitchen into account when working with sourdough. Our recipes are tested in a kitchen that is 68°F (20°C). If your kitchen is warmer, you will need to reduce your rising time in the first and second rise to avoid over-proving the dough.

If you'd like to prepare the dough and bake the rolls at a later time, after shaping the rolls in step 4, cover the dish with plastic wrap and store in the fridge for up to 36 hours. When ready to bake, allow them to have the second rise at room temperature until puffy and proceed with baking.

If using a tin baking sheet bake rolls at 400°F. Rolls can also be baked in a muffin tin for 23-25 minutes.

homemade croutons

PREP TIME: 10 mins - COOK TIME: 20 mins

Ingredients

1 loaf sourdough bread (or bread of your choice)
¼ cup extra virgin olive oil
½ teaspoon salt
¼ teaspoon black pepper
1 teaspoon garlic powder (optional)
1 teaspoon Italian seasoning (optional)

Instructions

OVEN INSTRUCTIONS
Preheat your oven to 375°F (190°C) and line a baking sheet with parchment paper.
Slice the bread into ¾" cubes and place them into a mixing bowl. Toss the cubes with the olive oil and seasonings. Spread them in an even layer on the baking sheet.

Bake for 20 minutes or until crispy and golden brown. Make sure to toss them halfway through the baking time. (This could take more or less time depending on how thick and dry your bread is.)

AIR FRYER INSTRUCTIONS
After coating the bread cubes with oil and seasonings, arrange them in a single layer on the air fryer tray. Cook at 375°F (190°C) for 4 minutes, toss with a spatula and cook for an additional 2-4 minutes.

sweet potato rolls

PREP TIME: 20 mins · COOK TIME: 20 mins · RISING TIME: 6 hrs

Ingredients

INGREDIENTS TO MAKE ½ CUP (100G) OF ACTIVE SOURDOUGH STARTER
1 tablespoon (15 g) sourdough starter
⅓ cup + 1 tablespoon (50 g) all-purpose flour
3 ½ tablespoons (50 g) water

DOUGH INGREDIENTS
1 ½ cups (300 g) mashed sweet potatoes (about 2 large sweet potatoes)
4 tablespoons (56 g) melted butter
½ cup (100 g) light brown sugar
1 ½ teaspoons (10 g) salt
½ cup (120 g) milk
1 large egg
½ cup (100 g) active sourdough starter
4 ⅓ cups plus 2 tablespoons (540 g) all-purpose flour

Instructions

FEED YOUR SOURDOUGH STARTER

12 hours before you plan to mix the dough, add the ingredients to make ½ cup (100 g) of active sourdough starter to a clean jar. Stir until combined, loosely cover the jar and let the starter rise at room temperature. (Or you can mix this in the bowl you plan to mix your dough in.) The sourdough starter is ready to use when it has doubled in size and there are plenty of bubbles on the surface and sides of the jar.

PREPARE SWEET POTATOES

Wash the sweet potatoes and pierce the flesh with a fork in several places. Place the sweet potatoes on a microwave-safe plate along with a cup filled halfway with water. Microwave on high until the flesh is easily pierced with a fork, about 10 minutes. Once the potatoes are cool enough to handle, remove the skins and mash the flesh. I used a potato ricer to get a smooth consistency. Add the butter to the sweet potatoes and stir to melt the butter and bring down the temperature of the potatoes.

MAKE THE DOUGH

Mix the dough. To a large mixing bowl, add the active sourdough starter, milk, egg, salt, light brown sugar and mashed sweet potatoes. Use a stiff spatula to mix the ingredients until well combined. Add the flour and mix it into the wet ingredients. You may need to switch to your hands to make sure all of the dry bits left in the bowl are incorporated into the dough. Cover the dough and let rest for one hour.

KNEAD THE DOUGH AND FIRST RISE

Turn the dough out onto a lightly floured surface and gently knead it for about 30-60 seconds or until the dough comes together into a smooth ball.

Place the dough back into the bowl, cover and allow it to rest at room temperature until risen 75% in size. (In my 68°F (20°C) kitchen, this takes about 8-9 hours. Adjust rising time according to your kitchens temperature. Cold temps need longer to rise, warmer temps need less time to rise.)

SECOND RISE IN FRIDGE

Place the bowl of dough in the fridge and let chill until ready to bake the next day. (The dough can be shaped and baked at this point if you do not wish to ferment longer in the fridge. Please note that the dough will be a little stickier to work with if it is not cold.)

SHAPE AND FINAL RISE

Line two baking sheets with parchment paper or a silicone baking mat.

Divide the dough. About 3 hours before you are ready to serve the rolls, take the dough out of the fridge and turn it out onto a floured surface. Work quickly to divide the dough into 12 equal portions that weigh about 104g each.

Shape each portion into a ball. Working with one portion at a time, use your hand to flatten the dough onto the work surface. Pull the sides of the dough into the center, turn it over and use your hands to twist the dough on the surface to form a ball. Press the ball into into a disc shape.

Final rise. Place 6 dough balls onto each sheet, spacing them 3" apart. Cover with a clean towel and allow the dough to rest at room temperature for 2-3 hours or until the dough becomes puffy.

Preheat your oven to 400°F (204°C). Bake one sheet of rolls at a time for 20-22 minutes. Remove from the oven and serve warm.

sourdough hamburger buns

PREP TIME: 10 mins · COOK TIME: 30 mins · RISING TIME: 6 hrs

Ingredients

INGREDIENTS TO MAKE ½ CUP (100G) OF ACTIVE SOURDOUGH STARTER
1 tablespoon (15 g) sourdough starter
⅓ cup + 1 tablespoon (50 g) all-purpose flour
3 ½ tablespoons (50 g) water

DOUGH INGREDIENTS
1 ½ cups (300 g) mashed sweet potatoes (about 2 large sweet potatoes)
4 tablespoons (56 g) melted butter
½ cup (100 g) light brown sugar
1 ½ teaspoons (10 g) salt
½ cup (120 g) milk
1 large egg
½ cup (100 g) active sourdough starter
4 ⅓ cups plus 2 tablespoons (540 g) all-purpose flour

Instructions

FEED YOUR SOURDOUGH STARTER
12 hours before you plan to mix the dough, add the ingredients to make ½ cup (100 g) of active sourdough starter to a clean jar. Stir until combined, loosely cover the jar and let the starter rise at room temperature. (Or you can mix this in the bowl you plan to mix your dough in.) The sourdough starter is ready to use when it has doubled in size and there are plenty of bubbles on the surface and sides of the jar.

30

(The ingredients will create a total of 60 g active starter but some of it will stick to the sides of the jar during the transfer, so we are making a little more than needed.)

MIX THE DOUGH
Add the ingredients to a large mixing bowl and use a spatula or your hands to mix them together until there are no dry bits in the bottom of the bowl. Cover the bowl and allow the dough to rest on the counter for 30 minutes.

PERFORM 3 SETS OF STRETCH AND FOLDS
Wet your hand with a little water to prevent sticking. Pick up the dough on one side and stretch it up and over itself. Turn the bowl a quarter turn and repeat this step until you have turned the bowl a full circle. The dough should form into a tight ball.
Cover the bowl and let the dough rest for 30 minutes.
Repeat the stretch and fold process two more times.

FIRST RISE
Cover the bowl and allow the dough to rise until doubled. (This took 6 hours in my 72°F (22°C) kitchen.)
After the dough has doubled, you can place the dough in the fridge for up to 2 days to bake them later OR proceed to the next step.

SHAPE AND SECOND RISE

Turn the dough out onto a floured surface. Divide the dough into 6 equal portions of 112-115 grams each.

Working with one portion at a time, shape the dough into a ball. Lightly flour the top of the dough and then place it on a parchment paper lined baking sheet. Repeat with the remaining dough.

Cover the sheet with a clean kitchen towel and allow the buns to rise at room temperature until puffy, 1-2 hours.

BAKE

Preheat your oven to 375°F (190°C). Mix the egg with the water in a small bowl and lightly brush the top of each dough ball. Sprinkle sesame seeds on top if desired. Bake for 25 minutes or until the buns are golden brown.

Remove the buns from the oven and allow them to cool before slicing.

einkorn sourdough bread

PREP TIME: 25 mins · COOK TIME: 40 mins · RISING TIME: 5 hrs

Ingredients

INGREDIENTS TO MAKE 1 CUP (200 G) OF ACTIVE SOURDOUGH STARTER

1 ½ tablespoons (25 g) sourdough starter
¾ cup + 1 tablespoon (100 g) all-purpose einkorn flour
7 tablespoons (100 g) water

DOUGH INGREDIENTS
1 cup (200 g) active sourdough starter
1 ¼ cup (300 g) water
4 ⅕ cups (540 g) all-purpose einkorn flour
2 teaspoons (10 g) sea salt

Instructions

FEED YOUR SOURDOUGH STARTER

12 hours before you plan to mix the dough, add the ingredients to make 1 cup (200 g) of active sourdough starter to a clean jar: 25g sourdough starter, 100g einkorn all-purpose flour and 100g water. Stir until combined, loosely cover the jar and let the starter rise at room temperature.

(The ingredients will create a total of 225 g active starter but, because some of it will stick to the sides of the jar during the transfer, we are making a little more than needed.)

The sourdough starter is ready to use when it has doubled in size and there are plenty of bubbles on the surface and sides of the jar.

MAKE THE DOUGH

Mix the dough ingredients. Add the 200g active sourdough starter, 540g all-purpose einkorn flour, 300g water and 10g salt to a large mixing bowl.

Use a dough whisk or an off-set spatula to mix the ingredients together until there are no dry bits left in the bowl. Cover the bowl and let the dough rest for 1 hour.

Fold the dough. Use a bowl scraper to turn the dough out onto a floured work surface. Flour the top of the dough and use your fingers to gently press it out into a rectangular shape.

Starting with one side of the dough, lift it up and fold it toward the center of the dough. If the dough is sticking to the work surface, use the bench scraper to help it release. Repeat this on all four sides of the dough and place the dough back into the bowl. Cover the bowl and let the dough rest for 15 minutes. Repeat the folding process one more time.

First rise. Place the dough back into the bowl and cover. Allow the dough to rise at room temperature for 3-4 hours or until it has risen by 20-30%.

Shape the dough. Turn the dough out onto a floured surface. Pull the sides of the dough into the middle, working all the way around the outside and then flip the dough over. Use your hands to cup the dough around the bottom near the work surface and turn it so that the dough forms a taut ball.

Second rise. Place the dough, seam-side up in to a floured banneton or one lined with a clean tea towel. Cover the dough and allow to rise at room temperature. Set a timer for 30 minutes.

When the timer goes off, turn on the oven to preheat to 500°F (260 °C) with the dutch oven inside. Set a timer for 1 hour and allow the oven to preheat for the final hour of the second rise.

(The dough will rise for a total of 1 hour and 30 minutes.)

Score the dough. Remove the dutch oven and set on top of your stove. Turn the dough out onto a piece of parchment paper. Score the top of the dough with a razor or sharp knife no deeper than ¼".

Use the parchment paper like a sling to transfer the dough to the dutch oven. Cover with the lid and place it back into the oven. Turn the oven down to 450°F (232 °C)

Bake for 40 minutes with the lid on. Remove the lid and check to see if the crust is dark enough to your liking. If it is, remove it and let cool. If not, bake for an additional 5-10 minutes uncovered.

Cool. Allow the bread to cool for 2 hours before slicing.

sourdough hawaiian rolls

PREP TIME: 15 mins - COOK TIME: 30 mins - RISING TIME: 12 hrs

Ingredients

INGREDIENTS TO MAKE ½ CUP (100 G) OF ACTIVE SOURDOUGH STARTER
1 tablespoon (15 g) sourdough starter
⅓ cup + 1 tablespoon (50 g) all-purpose flour
3 ½ tablespoons (50) water

DOUGH INGREDIENTS
2 tablespoons (28 g) butter
1 cup (240 g) pineapple juice
¼ cup (60 g) milk
3 tablespoons (36 g) sugar
1 ½ teaspoons (8 g) salt
½ cup (100 g) active sourdough starter
3 ⅔ cups (440 g) bread flour

EGG WASH
1 large egg (lightly beaten)

Instructions

FEED YOUR STARTER
12 hours before you plan to mix the dough, add the ingredients to make ½ cup (100 g) of

active sourdough starter to a clean jar. Stir until combined, loosely cover the jar and
starter rise at room temperature. (The ingredients will create a total of 115 g active star...
but, because some of it will stick to the sides of the jar during the transfer, we are making a
little more than needed.) The sourdough starter is ready to use when it has doubled in size
and there are plenty of bubbles on the surface and sides of the jar.

MAKE THE DOUGH

Melt butter: In a small saucepan, melt the butter, pineapple juice, milk, sugar and salt
together over low heat. Pour the mixture into the bowl of a stand mixer. Allow the liquid to
cool down to room temperature.

Mix the remaining dough ingredients: Add the flour and active sourdough starter to the
bowl and stir with a spatula until the ingredients are combined and there are no dry bits
left in the bowl. Cover the bowl and allow to rest at room temperature for 1 hour.

Stand Mix and First rise: Using the dough hook attachment, mix the dough on speed #1 for
8 minutes. Cover the bowl and allow the dough to rise at room temperature until it has
risen by 50% in size.

Shape: Turn the dough out onto a floured surface and divide it into 12 pieces,
approximately 74 grams each. Shape each piece into a ball by gathering up the sides and
pinching them together. Turn the dough over so that the seam side is down on the work
surface and gently form a smooth ball. Arrange them in a lightly greased glass baking dish.

Second rise: Cover the dish with a tea towel and let rise for 3-4 hours or until puffy.

Bake: About 20 minutes before you are ready to bake preheat your oven to 375°F (190°C).
Brush the top of the dough with the lightly beaten egg. Bake for 25-30 minutes or until they
are golden brown on top. The internal temperature of the rolls should be 190°F when fully
baked.

sourdough country loaf

PREP TIME: 40 mins · COOK TIME: 50 mins · RISING TIME: 12 hrs

Ingredients

INGREDIENTS TO MAKE ½ CUP (100 G) OF ACTIVE SOURDOUGH STARTER
1 tablespoon (15 g) sourdough starter
⅓ cup + 1 tablespoon (50 g) all-purpose flour
3 ½ tablespoons (50 g) water

DOUGH INGREDIENTS
½ cup (100 g) active sourdough starter
1 ½ cups (360 g) water (30 grams divided)
⅓ cup + 1 tablespoon (50 g) whole wheat flour
3 ¾ cups (450 g) bread flour
2 teaspoons (10 g) fine sea salt

Instructions

FEED YOUR SOURDOUGH STARTER
12 hours before you plan to mix the dough, add the ingredients to make ½ cup (100 g) of active sourdough starter to a clean jar. Stir until combined, loosely cover the jar and let the starter rise at room temperature. (The ingredients will create a total of 115 g active starter but, because some of it will stick to the sides of the jar during the transfer, we are making a little more than needed.) The sourdough starter is ready to use when it has doubled in size and there are plenty of bubbles on the surface and sides of the jar.

MAKE THE DOUGH

Autolyse (1 hour): In a mixing bowl, add 330 grams of water and 100 grams active sourdough starter, stir to combine. Add 50 grams whole wheat flour and 450 grams bread flour and use your hands to combine the ingredients until there are no dry bits and the dough looks like a shaggy mass. Cover the bowl and let the dough rest on the counter for 1 hour.

Add salt (1 hour): Add 10 grams of salt to 30 grams of water in a small bowl and stir to dissolve. Add the salt water to the dough and use your hands to work it in until well combined. Cover the bowl and let rest on the counter for 1 hour.

Bulk Fermentation (3-5.5 hours): Perform 3 sets of stretch and folds, 30 minutes apart. To perform a set, while the dough is still in the bowl, pick up one side with a wet hand. Pull it up and over itself. Turn the bowl and repeat this action on 4 sides of the dough until the bowl has come full circle. (See notes)

Cover the dough and allow to ferment at room temperature for 1-3 more hours according to the following temperatures.

68°F (20°C) 2-3 hours

70°F (21°C) 2-2.5 hours

72°F (22°C) 1.5-2 hours

75°F (24°C) 1-1.5 hours

The dough is ready for shaping when it has risen about 20-30% and has bubbles around the edges of the bowl.

Shaping: Turn the dough out onto a lightly floured surface and use a bench scraper to form it into a loose ball. Cover and let rest for 20 minutes.

Lightly flour the surface of the dough ball and use a bench scraper to turn it over. Final shape the dough by pulling the side nearest yourself up and towards the center of the dough. Repeat on all fours sides of the dough.

Flip the dough over, seam-side down, and use your hands to twist the dough on the counter. Cup the dough with your hands and gently pull it towards yourself to create a tight skin on the outside.

Flour the outside of the dough ball. Flour the inside of a banneton and place the dough ball into the banneton, seam-side up. Cover the bowl with a large plastic bag and let rest on the counter for 30 minutes.

Second Rise (8-36 hours): Place the covered dough in fridge to cold ferment 8-36 hours.

Score and Bake: Remove the dough from the fridge and let sit at room temperature for 30 minutes. Preheat the oven, with the dutch oven inside, to 500°F (260°C) for 30 minutes. Turn the dough out onto a piece of parchment paper and score the top with a razor. Remove the dutch oven and place on stove-top. Use the parchment paper as a sling and lift the dough up and into the dutch oven.

Cover, turn oven down to 450°F (232°C) and bake for 20 minutes. Remove the cover and bake an additional 25-30 minutes or until the crust is at the desired color.

Let the bread cool on a cooling rack for 2 hours before cutting.

soft sourdough pretzels

PREP TIME: 25 mins · COOK TIME: 14 mins · RISING TIME: 12 hrs

Ingredients

INGREDIENTS TO MAKE ½ CUP (100 G) OF ACTIVE SOURDOUGH STARTER
1 tablespoon (15 g) sourdough starter
⅓ cup + 1 tablespoon (50 g) all-purpose flour
3 ½ tablespoons (50 g) water

SOURDOUGH PRETZEL DOUGH
½ cup (100 g) active sourdough starter
1 cup plus 1 tablespoon (255 g) water
2 tablespoons (40 g) honey (or sugar)
2 teaspoons (10 g) fine sea salt
4 cups + 2 tablespoons (500 g) bread flour

WATER BATH
6 cups water
2 tablespoons baking soda
1 tablespoon dark brown sugar

EGG WASH
1 large egg (lightly beaten in a small bowl)
1 tablespoon coarse salt

Instructions

FEED YOUR SOURDOUGH STARTER

12 hours before you plan to mix the dough, add the ingredients to make ½ cup (100 g) of active sourdough starter to a clean jar. Stir until combined, loosely cover the jar and let the starter rise at room temperature. (The ingredients will create a total of 115 g active starter but, because some of it will stick to the sides of the jar during the transfer, we are making a little more than needed.) The sourdough starter is ready to use when it has doubled in size and there are plenty of bubbles on the surface and sides of the jar.

MAKE THE DOUGH

In the bowl of a stand mixer, stir together the active sourdough starter, water, honey and salt with a spatula. Add the bread flour and use your hands to bring the ingredients together as best as possible. The dough will be very stiff. Place the dough hook on the mixer and mix the dough on the lowest speed for 6-7 minutes. (Or knead by hand for 10 minutes.) Cover the bowl and let rest at room temperature for 8-12 hours.
Line a baking sheet with parchment paper. Turn the dough out onto a clean work surface and divide into 16 equal pieces.

Working one piece at a time, roll the dough into a long rope shape and set it on a clean surface in the shape of a "U". Lift the ends of the rope and twist 2 times. Fold the twist over and press the ends on the dough. Cover the dough with a towel and let rise for 30-60 minutes or until puffy.
Preheat oven to 425°F (218°C) making sure that the oven rack in the center position. Boil the water in a large stockpot and add 2 tablespoons baking soda and 1 tablespoon of dark brown sugar.
Boil the pretzels, 3-4 at a time, on both sides for 30 seconds each, making sure not to crowd the pot. Use a mesh stainer to remove the pretzels and place back on the parchment paper. Brush each pretzel with egg wash and sprinkle with salt.
Bake the pretzels at 425°F (218°C) for 12-14 minutes or until golden brown.

pull apart cheese bread

PREP TIME: 10 mins - COOK TIME: 40 mins

Ingredients

1 loaf crusty bread (sourdough or Italian)
8 tablespoons butter
1 tablespoon garlic powder
2 tablespoons chopped parsley
½ cup grated parmesan cheese
2 cups shredded mozzarella cheese
1 cup marinara sauce (or pizza sauce for dipping)

Instructions

Preheat your oven to 375°F (190°C).
Using a sharp, serrated knife, cut a diamond pattern into the top of the bread making sure that the knife doesn't go all the way through to the bottom of the loaf. Each slice should be about an inch wide. Place a piece of foil on top of a baking sheet and place the loaf onto the foil.
In a small saucepan, melt the butter and stir in the garlic powder. Remove from the heat and use a pastry brush to coat the cracks and exterior of the bread. Fill the cracks with shredded cheese and parsley and wrap the loaf in the foil.
Bake the loaf for 30 minutes, unwrap the top of the loaf and bake an additional 10 minutes. Serve immediately.

slow cooker
sourdough bread

PREP TIME: 30 mins · COOK TIME: 2 hrs · FERMENTING TIME: 6 hrs

Ingredients

INGREDIENTS TO MAKE ½ CUP (100 G) OF ACTIVE SOURDOUGH STARTER
1 tablespoon (15 g) sourdough starter
⅓ cup + 1 tablespoon (50 g) all-purpose flour
3 ½ tablespoons (50 g) water

DOUGH INGREDIENTS
½ cup (100 g) active sourdough starter
1 ⅓ cups + 2 tablespoons (350 g) water
⅓ cup + 1 tablespoon (50 g) whole wheat flour
3 ¾ cups (450 g) bread flour
2 teaspoons (10 g) fine sea salt

Instructions

FEED YOUR SOURDOUGH STARTER
12 hours before you plan to mix the dough, add the ingredients to make ½ cup (100 g) of active sourdough starter to a clean jar. Stir until combined, loosely cover the jar and let the starter rise at room temperature. (The ingredients will create a total of 115 g active starter but, because some of it will stick to the sides of the jar during the transfer, we are making a little more than needed.) The sourdough starter is ready to use when it has doubled in size and there are plenty of bubbles on the surface and sides of the jar.

MAKE THE DOUGH
Mix Dough Ingredients: Add the ingredients to a large mixing bowl. Use your hands to combine the ingredients until there are no dry bits and the dough looks like a shaggy mass. Cover the bowl and let the dough rest on the counter for 1 hour.

Stretch and fold: Perform 3 sets of stretches and folds, 30 minutes apart. To perform a set, while the dough is still in the bowl, pick up one side with a wet hand. Pull it up and over itself. Turn the bowl and repeat this action on 4 sides of the dough until the bowl has come full circle. Cover the dough and allow to ferment at room temperature according to the following temperatures.
68 - 70°F (20 - 21°C) 2 - 2 ½ hours
72 - 75°F (22 - 24°C) 1- 1 ½ hours
The dough is ready for shaping when it has risen about 20-30% and has bubbles around the edges of the bowl.

Shaping: Turn the dough out onto a lightly floured surface and use a bench scraper to form it into a loose ball. Cover and let rest for 20 minutes.

Lightly flour the surface of the dough ball and use a bench scraper to turn it over. Final shape the dough by pulling the side nearest yourself up and towards the center of the dough. Repeat on all fours sides of the dough.

Flip the dough over, seam-side down, and use your hands to twist the dough on the counter. Cup the dough with your hands and gently pull it towards yourself to create a tight skin on the outside.

Flour the outside of the dough ball. Flour the inside of a banneton and place the dough ball into the banneton, seam-side up. Cover the bowl with a large plastic bag and let rest on the counter for 1 - ½ hours.

Slow Cook: Lightly spray the inside of your slow cooker with cooking spray. Turn the dough out onto a piece of parchment paper and place it into the slow cooker. Turn the slow cooker onto the HIGH setting and allow to slow cook for 1 hour.

Cool: Check the internal temperature of the bread using a digital food thermometer. It is done when it registers at least 200°F (93°C). Remove the bread from the slow cooker and cool on a cooling rack for 2 hours before cutting. (If you would like a darker crust, place the bread under the oven broiler until it reaches desired color.)

53

sourdough french toast

PREP TIME: 5 mins - COOK TIME: 8 mins

Ingredients
6 slices sourdough bread (¾" thick)
2 tablespoons (28 g) butter
2 tablespoons (30 g) vegetable oil
CUSTARD INGREDIENTS
3 large eggs
1 cup (240 g) heavy cream
¼ teaspoon (2 g) fine sea salt
½ teaspoon (3 g) ground cinnamon
¼ teaspoon (2 g) ground nutmeg
2 tablespoons (30 g) white sugar
1 teaspoon (5 g) vanilla extract

Instructions

Preheat oven to 400° and place a baking sheet inside. Heat skillet over medium-low heat with the butter and oil.
Use a whisk to combine the eggs, heavy cream, sugar, vanilla extract, cinnamon, nutmeg and salt in a bowl. Pour the custard mixture into a shallow baking dish. Soak 2 slices of bread 10 minutes on each side.
Cook the slices on the 3-4 minutes per side. (Place the next 2 slices in the custard to soak while the current slices are cooking.) Transfer to the oven on the baking sheet to keep them warm until you are ready to serve.

54

sourdough english muffins

PREP TIME: 20 mins - COOK TIME: 8 mins - TOTAL TIME: 1 day

Ingredients

INGREDIENTS TO MAKE ½ CUP (100 G) OF ACTIVE SOURDOUGH STARTER
1 tablespoon (15 g) sourdough starter
⅓ cup + 1 tablespoon (50 g) all-purpose flour
3 ½ tablespoons (50) water

DOUGH INGREDIENTS
½ cup (100 g) active sourdough starter
1 tablespoon (20 g) honey (sugar or maple syrup)
1 cup (240 g) milk
3 cups (360 g) all-purpose flour
1 teaspoon (5 g) fine sea salt
¼ cup (40 g) cornmeal (for sprinkling)

Instructions

FEED YOUR SOURDOUGH STARTER
12 hours before you plan to mix the dough, add the ingredients to make ½ cup (100 g) of active sourdough starter to a clean jar. Stir until combined, loosely cover the jar and let the starter rise at room temperature. (The ingredients will create a total of 115 g active starter but, because some of it will stick to the sides of the jar during the transfer, we are making a little more than needed.) The sourdough starter is ready to use when it has doubled in size and there are plenty of bubbles on the surface and sides of the jar.

MAKE THE DOUGH

Add 100g of the active starter and the rest of the ingredients (except corn meal) to a large bowl and use your hands to mix until well combined. Cover and let rest 30-60 minutes. Turn the dough out onto a floured surface and knead the dough by hand for 5 minutes. (A stand mixer with a dough hook attachment can be used on the lowest speed.)
Place the dough back into the bowl, cover and let ferment on the counter at room temperature 8-12 hours. (Room temperature is 65-70°F)

CUT AND COOK

Turn the dough out onto a floured surface, flour the top of the dough and press it out using your fingertips until it is 1" in thickness.
Use a 3" biscuit cutter to cut rounds and place them on a parchment lined baking sheet that's been sprinkled with cornmeal. Sprinkle the tops with cornmeal, cover with a tea towel and allow to rise for 1 hour at room temperature.
Preheat your non-stick skillet over LOW heat. Place 4 muffins into the skillet spaced 2" apart, cover and cook the first side for 4 minutes. Turn the muffins over and cook for an additional 4 minutes. (When done, the center of a muffin should register about 200°F on an instant-read thermometer.)

Notes

Use the scoop and level technique to measure your flour if you do not have a kitchen scale. To do this, use a spoon to fluff up the flour in the bag. Use a spoon to scoop the flour into a measuring cup until it is heaped on top. Take a butterknife and level off the top. This should give you the most accurate measurement for flour.

If you live in a very warm or humid environment, you may need to make adjustments in the recipe.

honey wheat sourdough sandwich bread

PREP TIME: 15 mins · COOK TIME: 45 mins · REST: 9 hrs

Ingredients

INGREDIENTS TO MAKE ½ CUP ACTIVE SOURDOUGH STARTER
1 tablespoon (15 g) sourdough starter
⅓ cup + 1 tablespoon (50 g) all-purpose flour
3 ½ tablespoons (50 g) water

DOUGH INGREDIENTS
½ cup (100 g) active sourdough starter
1 ⅓ cup + 1 teaspoon (325 g) water
2 tablespoons (40 g) honey
2 tablespoons (30 g) olive oil
2 teaspoons (10 g) sea salt
1 cup + 1 teaspoon (125 g) whole wheat flour
3 cups + 2 tablespoons (375 g) bread flour

Instructions

FEED YOUR SOURDOUGH STARTER
12 hours before you plan to mix the dough, add the ingredients to make ½ cup (100 g) of active sourdough starter to a clean jar. Stir until combined, loosely cover the jar and let the starter rise at room temperature.

59

(The ingredients will create a total of 115 g active starter but, because some of it will stick to the sides of the jar during the transfer, we are making a little more than needed.) The sourdough starter is ready to use when it has doubled in size and there are plenty of bubbles on the surface and sides of the jar.

MAKE THE DOUGH

8 AM - Mix the dough: To a large mixing bowl, add ½ cup (100 g) of active sourdough starter, water, honey, olive oil and sea salt. Use a stiff spatula to stir the ingredients. Add the bread flour and whole wheat flour to the bowl and stir with the spatula. Switch to your hands and mix the dough until it resembles a shaggy mess and there are no dry bits in the bowl. Cover the bowl and let the dough rest for 1 hour.

9 AM - First rise: Wet your hand with water and stretch and fold the dough until it tightens up and starts to form a ball. Turn the dough in the bowl until it's slightly smooth on the outside. Cover the bowl and allow the dough to rise at room temperature, 68-72°F (20-22°C), for 3-4 hours or until it has risen by about 30-50%.

1 PM - Shape and second rise: Turn the dough out onto a lightly floured surface and gently press it into a rectangular shape. Fold the two longest sides inwards about 1 inch. Fold the short side towards the opposite end until the loaf resembles a log shape. Place the dough seam-side down in a lightly greased 9" x 5" loaf pan. Allow the dough to rest at room temperature, uncovered until the dough has risen to the rim of the pan, about 3-4 hours.

5 PM - Bake: Preheat the oven to 375°F (190°C) and bake for 45 minutes. Allow the bread to cool in the pan for 10-15 minutes before transferring to a cooling rack.

Notes
To store: Store the bread in a bread bag, beeswax wrap or kitchen towel at room temperature. The loaf will keep fresh for a few days.
To freeze: Wrap individual loaves in plastic wrap and insert into a freezer-safe container. Make sure they have cooled completely before wrapping.

sourdough ciabatta rolls

PREP TIME: 15 mins · COOK TIME: 30 mins · TOTAL TIME: 12 hrs

Ingredients

INGREDIENTS TO MAKE ½ CUP (100 G) OF ACTIVE SOURDOUGH STARTER
1 tablespoon (15 g) sourdough starter
⅓ cup + 1 tablespoon (50 g) all-purpose flour
3 ½ tablespoons (50 g) water

CIABATTA DOUGH INGREDIENTS
½ cup (100 g) active sourdough starter
4 cups + 2 tablespoons (500 g) bread flour
1 ⅔ cups (400 g) water
2 teaspoons (10 g) salt

Instructions

FEED YOUR SOURDOUGH STARTER
12 hours before you plan to mix the dough, add the ingredients to make ½ cup (100 g) of active sourdough starter to a clean jar. Stir until combined, loosely cover the jar and let the starter rise at room temperature. (The ingredients will create a total of 115 g active starter but, because some of it will stick to the sides of the jar during the transfer, we are making a little more than needed.) The sourdough starter is ready to use when it has doubled in size and there are plenty of bubbles on the surface and sides of the jar.

MAKE THE DOUGH

Mix the dough. Combine the active sourdough starter, bread flour, water and salt in a large mixing bowl. Use a stiff spatula or your hands to incorporate the ingredients, making sure there are no dry bits left in the bowl. Cover the bowl and let the dough rest at room temperature for 1 hour.

Stretch and fold. Perform 3 sets of stretches and folds, 30 minutes apart. Keep the bowl covered in between each set.

First rise. Cover the dish and allow the dough to rise about 50% in volume,. This can take anywhere from 3-6 hours at room temperature. Warm kitchens will take less time, cold kitchens will need more time. See notes for rising times.

Second rise. Place the covered bowl of dough in the fridge for 8-36 hours for a long ferment OR proceed to the next step and shape the dough.

Shape. Remove the dough from the fridge and generously flour your work surface before turning the dough out onto it. Flour the top of the dough and use your hands to form it into a rectangular shape. Be careful not to press the air from the dough. Cut the dough into 8 pieces and place them on a parchment lined baking sheet. Cover with a clean towel and allow the dough to rise at room temperature for 2 hours or until puffy.

Bake. While the dough is resting, preheat your oven to 475°F (246°C). Bake the ciabatta dough for 10 minutes, turn the oven down to 425°F (218°C) and bake for an additional 20 minutes or until the crust is a deep golden brown. Allow the ciabatta bread to cool on a cooling rack for 30 minutes before slicing.

Notes

On our final testing for this recipe, our kitchen was 72°F (22°C) and it took 3 hours for our dough to rise to 50% in volume during the first rise (step 3).

At 70°F (21°C) check around 3 ½ hours and at 68°F (20°C) check around 4 hours.

These times also depend on the strength of your sourdough starter. Please note that these times are only a reference to help you so that you do not overproof the dough. Results will vary in EVERY kitchen.

64

sourdough berry sweet rolls

PREP TIME: 10 mins · COOK TIME: 35 mins · TOTAL TIME: 10 hrs

Ingredients

INGREDIENTS TO MAKE 100G (½ CUP) OF ACTIVE SOURDOUGH STARTER
1 tablespoon (15 g) sourdough starter
⅓ cup + 1 tablespoon (50 g) all-purpose flour
3 ½ tablespoons (50) water
DOUGH INGREDIENTS
½ cup (100 g) active sourdough starter
8 tablespoons (113 g) unsalted butter (cold)
4 cups (480 g) all-purpose flour
1 cup (240 g) milk, 2 tablespoons (25 g) sugar
1 teaspoon (5 g) salt
BERRY FILLING
2 ½ cups (387.5 g) frozen or fresh berries (chop larger pieces)
½ cup (100 g) granulated sugar
2 teaspoons all-purpose flour
zest of one lemon
½ teaspoon ground cinnamon
GLAZE
1 cup (120 g) powdered sugar
1 tablespoon (14 g) melted butter
1 teaspoon (5 g) vanilla extract
1 tablespoon lemon juice
1 tablespoon (30 g) milk

65

Instructions

FEED YOUR SOURDOUGH STARTER

12 hours before you plan to mix the dough, add the ingredients to make ½ cup (100 g) of active sourdough starter to a clean jar. Stir until combined, loosely cover the jar and let the starter rise at room temperature. (The ingredients will create a total of 115 g active starter but, because some of it will stick to the sides of the jar during the transfer, we are making a little more than needed.) The sourdough starter is ready to use when it has doubled in size and there are plenty of bubbles on the surface and sides of the jar.

MAKE THE DOUGH AND FIRST RISE

Use a cheese grater to grate the cold butter into a mixing bowl. Add the flour and use a fork to toss with the butter. Add the active sourdough starter, milk, sugar and salt. Mix with a spatula until the ingredients are well incorporated and there are no dry bits in the bowl. Use your hands to help bring the dough together. Cover the bowl and let rest on the counter for 1 hour.

Knead the dough on the counter for 1 minute or until it is smooth. Cover the bowl and let rest on the counter for 8-10 hours. The dough should double in size.

SHAPE AND SECOND RISE

Place the sugar, flour, lemon zest and cinnamon in a bowl. Use a spatula to mix and set the bowl aside.

Flour your work surface and turn the dough onto it. Flour the top of the dough. Use a rolling pin to roll the dough into a 12" x 18" rectangle.

Spoon the sugar mixture evenly over the surface, leaving a half inch bare along the edges. Sprinkle the berries over the top. Starting on one side, roll the dough into a log shape. Use the bench-scraper to cut the log into 12 pieces (approximately 1.5 inches). Arrange the portions in a greased 9" x 13" baking dish.

Cover the rolls with a clean kitchen towel and allow them to come to room temperature and the berries to release their juices. This should take about 2 hours.

BAKE

Preheat the oven to 400°F (204°C). Bake the cinnamon rolls for 30 minutes or until the tops are golden brown. Remove and allow them to cool while you make the lemon glaze.

MAKE THE LEMON GLAZE

Combine the powdered sugar, lemon juice, melted butter and milk in a bowl. If the glaze is too thick, add a teaspoon of milk at a time to avoid over-thinning of the glaze. (If the glaze is too thin, add more powdered sugar to thicken it.)

Pour the glaze evenly over the top of the sweet rolls and serve warm.

gluten free sourdough bread

PREP TIME: 15 mins - COOK TIME: 1 hrs - RISING TIME: 4 hrs

Ingredients

INGREDIENTS TO MAKE 100G (½ CUP) OF ACTIVE SOURDOUGH STARTER
1 tablespoon (15 g) sourdough starter
⅓ cup + 1 tablespoon (50 g) all-purpose flour
3 ½ tablespoons (50) water
DOUGH INGREDIENTS
½ cup (100 g) active sourdough starter
8 tablespoons (113 g) unsalted butter (cold)
4 cups (480 g) all-purpose flour
1 cup (240 g) milk
2 tablespoons (25 g) sugar
1 teaspoon (5 g) salt
BERRY FILLING
2 ½ cups (387.5 g) frozen or fresh berries (chop larger pieces)
½ cup (100 g) granulated sugar
2 teaspoons all-purpose flour
zest of one lemon
½ teaspoon ground cinnamon
GLAZE
1 cup (120 g) powdered sugar
1 tablespoon (14 g) melted butter
1 teaspoon (5 g) vanilla extract
1 tablespoon lemon juice
1 tablespoon (30 g) milk

69

Instructions

FEED YOURFEED YOUR STARTER

12 hours before you plan to mix the dough, add the ingredients to make 1 cup (250 g) of active sourdough starter to a clean jar. Stir until combined, loosely cover the jar and let the starter rise at room temperature. The sourdough starter is ready to use when there are plenty of bubbles on the sides of the jar and the starter has risen by 25-30%.

MAKE THE DOUGH

Combine the water with the ground flax seeds, active gluten free sourdough starter, honey, olive oil, apple cider vinegar in a mixing bowl and set aside.

Combine the dry ingredients in the bowl of a stand mixer. Use the paddle attachment to mix them for 1 to 2 minutes making sure they are well incorporated. This step is very important.

Pour the wet ingredients into the bowl of the stand mixture with the dry ingredients.

Beat the dough on the lowest speed for 5 minutes, scrapping down the sides of the bowl as necessary. When you lift the paddle attachment, the dough should slowly fall off of the paddle. If it stays on the paddle, add 30 g of water at a time until you achieve the right consistency. The dough should be thick but not stiff.

RISE

Line a 9" x 5" baking tin with parchment paper. Pour the dough into the tin and use a spatula to spread it evenly.

Set your oven to the bread proofing setting. Allow the bread to rise in the oven for 3-4 hours or until it rises to the top of the baking tin. If your oven does not have this setting, let the oven preheat to its lowest temperature while you make the dough. Turn the oven off and allow the dough to rise in the oven. OR, cover the dough with a kitchen towel or plastic and allow to rise at room temperature until the dough has risen slightly higher than the top rim of the baking tin. This can take anywhere from 6-12 hours depending on the temperature of your kitchen.

BAKE

Remove the dough from the oven. Turn the oven on to 375°F (190°C). When the oven has come to temperature, score the top of the dough with a razor or sharp knife. Bake for 60 minutes.

Remove the bread from the baking pan and parchment paper immediately. If you do not remove the parchment paper, the bottom of the bread will become soggy. Allow the bread to cool on a cooling rack completely before cutting.

Store the bread at room temperature in a closed container for up to 3 days. Or freeze for up to 3 months.

Made in the USA
Columbia, SC
11 August 2024